John Arden

by

SIMON TRUSSLER

Columbia University Press

NEW YORK & LONDON 1973

COLUMBIA ESSAYS ON MODERN WRITERS
is a series of critical studies of English,
Continental, and other writers whose works are of contemporary
artistic and intellectual significance.

Editor

George Stade

Advisory Editors

Jacques Barzun   W. T. H. Jackson   Joseph A. Mazzeo

John Arden is Number 65 of the series

SIMON TRUSSLER
is an editor of *Theatre Quarterly* and theatre
critic of the London weekly review *Tribune*. His
full-length studies of the plays of John Osborne,
Arnold Wesker, John Whiting, and Harold Pinter
have been published in Britain by Gollancz, and
he is currently supervising a major revision of
The Oxford Companion to the Theatre.

Library of Congress Cataloging in Publication Data

Trussler, Simon.
  John Arden.

  (Columbia essays on modern writers, no. 65)
Bibliography: p. 47–48
1. Arden, John.   I. Series
PR6051.R3Z9   822′.9′14   72-13924
ISBN 0-231-03533-0

PR
6051
R3
Z9

John Arden

Closely identified though John Arden has become with the other young British playwrights who began writing in the late 1950s, his dramatic career has taken an entirely individual and in some ways disturbing direction. The controlled originality of his technique was the more remarkable at a time when John Osborne and Arnold Wesker, for all their uncompromising innovations in subject-matter, were still writing within conventional formal molds: and the unequivocal left-wing commitment of such writers contrasted strongly with the scrupulous balance of argumentative power in Arden's early plays. Yet in recent years Arden's professionalism has been diluted, in effect if not intention, by an almost exclusive involvement with community and fringe theatre groups—and this has itself reflected a shift in the political emphasis of his plays. Bolder and often cruder in outline, they have become more and more directly propagandist, yet at the same time simply less accessible (in any sense) to a wide playgoing public. Steadily increasing critical recognition, culminating in the accolade of a production of *Armstrong's Last Goodnight* at the National Theatre in 1965, fell away as Arden seemed to withdraw into a period of self-doubt and artistic uncertainty from which, as this essay goes to press, he may at last be emerging, with major productions of two new full-length plays planned in the next six months.

John Arden was born in the industrial Yorkshire town of Barnsley in 1930, and his roots have remained in the north country—which provides alike the bleak background for *Serjeant Musgrave's Dance* and the garish, local-political colors of *The Workhouse Donkey*. Unlike most of his generation of

[3]

dramatists (and most of the townsfolk of prewar Barnsley), Arden came from a relatively well-off family, and so received a public school education at Sedbergh: but the writing career he had decided to follow by the age of seventeen might not be best served, he felt, by his going on to read English at a university. Instead, he studied architecture—for three years at King's College, Cambridge, and later at Edinburgh College of Art. His admitted lack of flair for the practicalities of this profession gave the television play *Wet Fish* its genesis: but there is, all the same, a sense of proportion and a feeling for structural coherence in Arden's plays—especially in their interlocking of episodic elements and their attention to the scenic problems these pose —to which his apparently false start may have contributed. Arden has himself compared the "schedule of accommodation" which a client draws up for an architect with a playwright's approach to his plays: "You start, perhaps, with a story that divides itself naturally into half a dozen scenes—the rooms of the house—which you have to put together so that they work one from the other, and at the same time the thing has to make up a complete whole."

It is less clear whether Arden's reluctant admiration for the rougher traditions of soldiering derives from his two years of National Service, which he spent in the Intelligence Corps, although generally it is evident that his personal experiences have not provided more than incidental inspiration for his plays. These he had begun to write seriously and prolifically at sixteen, graduating from a work "based on the death of Hitler written in the style of *Samson Agonistes*" to his first performed play, a "Victorian piece, about the building of a railway, called *All Fall Down*," which was staged by Arden's college drama group while he was in Edinburgh. But it was his entries in two playwriting competitions that first brought him public recognition. The radio play *The Life of Man* won a BBC Northern Region prize in 1956, and this distinction, together with the short-listing of

[4]

The Waters of Babylon in *The Observer*'s play competition, encouraged Arden to approach the English Stage Company, recently formed at the Royal Court Theatre, and already building upon the success of Osborne's *Look Back in Anger*. *The Waters of Babylon* was given a one-night production without decor at the Court in 1957 and began Arden's fruitful association with that theatre. In the same year, he was commissioned by the English Stage Company to complete his second full-length play, *Live Like Pigs*, upon which he gave up his job in an architect's office. He has devoted himself full-time to writing ever since — as a Fellow in Playwriting at Bristol University in 1959–60 — and for much of his early career divided his time between the isolated Yorkshire village of Kirbymoorside and an even more remote retreat off the coast of Ireland.

During this period Arden enjoyed increasing critical esteem, but little box-office success. Although the early, exploratory plays he went on to write for the Royal Court — *Live Like Pigs* was staged there in 1958, with *Serjeant Musgrave's Dance* and *The Happy Haven* following in successive years — have probably become his best known and most widely performed works, at the time they were praised with faint damns by most of the critics; and it was in large part an idiosyncratic campaign waged in Arden's support by the little-theatre magazine *Encore* that kept discussion of his work alive, until productions on the university and repertory circuits began to change reviewers' minds. *The Workhouse Donkey* and *Armstrong's Last Goodnight,* both staged at the Chichester Festival playhouse during its brief period as a kind of out-of-town National Theatre in 1963–64, earned Arden a certain vicarious prestige, which was heightened when *Armstrong* was transferred to the Old Vic. But the response to *Left-Handed Liberty* — a play commissioned for the Mermaid Theatre by the City of London, to commemorate the anniversary of Magna Carta in 1965 — was a more characteristic mixture of hostility and bafflement.

[5]

The play itself marked the culmination of a second distinct period in Arden's work, during which his chief concern had been with *The Business of Good Government*—the title under which he had dramatized the Christmas story in 1960. It marked, too, the end of a period of remarkably sustained creative activity. Between 1957 and 1965 Arden had written fourteen plays, eight of them full-length works for the stage: in the next six years he was to write five, of which only one—*The Hero Rises Up,* staged briefly in a misconceived production by the author at the Round House in 1968—can be accounted of more than minor interest. By this time Arden had moved, with his wife and occasional collaborator, Margaretta D'Arcy, and their four children, to Muswell Hill in London—apparently in his continuing quest to discover the role of a playwright in his community, a quest which he obliquely dramatized in the radio play *The Bagman,* broadcast in 1970. The ambiguous ending of that play may or may not reflect the uncertainties of Arden's own search, for ambiguity has always been a feature of his work—usually the purposeful ambiguity inseparable from an honest refusal to offer easy answers.

In the earlier plays, in particular, Arden is determined to give every devil his due, and he does so by drawing analogies rather than blood. And if this is reminiscent of Shavian technique, it is all the more appropriate that John Arden's first stage play should have been, like Bernard Shaw's, about slum landlords. Indeed, there is a dash of *Mrs. Warren's Profession* besides a flavor of *Widowers' Houses* about *The Waters of Babylon* (1957): and it is interesting, too, that Arden's second play should have taken its title from Blanche Sartorius's outburst of contempt for the laboring classes—"those dirty, drunken disreputable people who live like pigs"—in *Widowers' Houses.* For Arden's approach to dramatizing a social problem is close to Shaw's, alike in his tangential way of touching upon the ethics of an issue and in his authorial attitude toward it. Underlying the refusal to simplify his work by cutting convenient polemical corners lies a deep moral consciousness and commitment.

Arden also shares with Shaw an interest, almost a preoccupation, with the intricacies and intrigues of municipal government. Just as Sartorius in *Widowers' Houses* protects his own interests as a member of the vestry, so Krank in *The Waters of Babylon* connives with that one-time party boss par excellence, Charlie Butterthwaite, to subvert the borough council he cannot beat. Krank is a Polish exile who leads a double life as a respectable architect by day and keeper of a disorderly lodging house by night; while Butterthwaite has been for nine years the Napoleon of his native northern city—but by the time *The Waters of Babylon* begins he too is a refugee in the anonymity of the metropolis. Both characters crop up again in several of Arden's later plays, and the author's evident fondness for the two rogues, as distinct from the evil they perpetrate in the cause of self-preservation, is as clear and unself-conscious as his deliberate coinage of comic-book names for them. Arden is a rarity among modern playwrights in preserving a clear distinction between the formal conventions of his comic and his serious writing: and *The Waters of Babylon* is in the broad, latter-day Aristophanic tradition that was later to erupt into *The Workhouse Donkey.*

The play is extravagently plotted, generously peopled—a scenically-shuttling kaleidoscope of down-at-heel London life in the early 1950s. Coincidence functions here not with the shyly intruding excuses of the well-made play but as a fine art in itself, a satisfaction of improbable expectations. And the characters, a racial mixture of Poles, English, Irish, and West Indians, embody in this comedy of contemporary humours many of the mythic archetypes of urban life, caught from an unexpected angle. Thus, Arden remolds one English folk-hero—the self-educated working man turned reforming councilor—into his own Charlie Butterthwaite, dedicated as much to lining his pockets as to the interests of his constituents. And from a stereotyped mid-century villain—the urban immigrant who bites not only the hands that have received him but those of his fellow seekers after a better life in a foreign land—he has created Krank, a kind of Father Courage whose misfortunes have taught him the necessity for battening on the misfortunes of others, and whose almost heroic quality consists in his very capacity for survival and, indeed, for hard work.

Only the three-act shape of the play—including the working-up toward strong curtains Arden no doubt felt obligatory—observes the formal dictates of those theatrical times; and there is a freedom from overspecific scenic impedimenta, as from the usual manufactured contiguities of characters and events in a single sitting-room, that is rare in plays of this period. The narrative progress of the work is surely controlled, its exposition unashamed; and the switches between colloquial dialogue, astringent song, and that whimsical, house-arrested free verse Arden has since made his own are purposeful in their inversion of idiomatic convention. Here it is the politics which tend to be poeticized, whereas matters of love or honor become common-sensically prosaic—indeed, the only set-speech in verse which touches on love is Krank's repudiation of it. "I must stand uninvolved" is the key to the "central European paradox" he embodies: and the play is for him a grotesque nightmare of hapless involvement, bringing about his downfall.

Charlie Butterthwaite—his own, quite different idiom a blend of habitual bonhomie, a kind of committee-room poetry and the truer lyricism of his recollected poverty—is Krank's equal and opposite, able to survive only within the labyrinthine social and political system he is a past-master at manipulating. Krank is a loner, Butterthwaite a leader. Krank thrives by pushing a system of *laissez faire* to its ultimate extreme, Butterthwaite by tying up bureaucracy's red tape to his own best advantage. And because their humours are incompatible, their collusion is doomed to fail—a point which it is necessary to stress, since it

[8]

gives drive and direction to an apparently discursive plot. It is true that the play's third act works least well, but this is due less to its pleasantly busy tying of loose ends than to a felt restrictiveness in its setting. The technical skill of the piece is at times stronger than its release of resultant energies into fruitful channels: but for a first play it remains a considerable achievement in its complete independence of manner and in its control over its own density of matter.

Soldier, Soldier was written in 1957, soon after *The Waters of Babylon,* though it was three years before a television production of it reached the screen. It is, nevertheless, clearly a product of the earliest period of Arden's creative career, whether in its method of interchanging prose and verse, or in its imposition of an outsize character upon an essentially small-time plot. Just as Krank and Butterthwaite cut their purposive ways through the back streets of Arden's modern Babylon, so the fusilier who strides into a seedy public bar at the beginning of this play virtually takes over the small corner of the northern colliery town whose thirst the tavern quenches. The soldier, never named, blows like a tipsy gale through the action, demolishing the tiny ambitions of the folk on whom he plays a callous confidence trick as of right—his own right to a comfortable subsistence.

If *The Waters of Babylon* explores the problems of municipal housing and of community relations in a lighter vein than *Live Like Pigs,* then *Soldier, Soldier* can be seen as an even-tempered trial run for the harsher and more demanding *Serjeant Musgrave's Dance.* In spite of the differences of season, century, and style, there is, as Arden has himself commented, the same "air of violence from the outside world coming in on a closed community." But *Soldier, Soldier* succeeds much less well in establishing self-consistent conventions for making its violence credible. The deception on which the plot depends is flimsy—scarcely more than an excuse, indeed, for exploring the reactions of a small-minded household to the presence of a larger-than-life scapegrace. And if the town's "general air of muck without much money" is clearly realized, in pub and domestic interiors much more specific than those of *The Waters of Babylon*, this only heightens one's feeling that *Soldier, Soldier* is a television play that would actually work better on stage—to which it could readily be adapted. Arden's own preface confesses, too, that the "increased intimacy" of television makes some of the poetic passages potentially embarrassing—though it is, in fact, largely in the monosyllabic vigor and forceful enjambments of the soldier's verse speeches that he compels attention. Flimsily rooted as this attention is in character or conviction, it is perhaps as tenuous a deception as the soldier's own.

Here, then, Arden's sense of situation—the townsfolk could have been carved out of their own paving stones, so impressed are they with the casual waywardness of everyday life—is much stronger than (and probably anticipated) the trappings of his plot. And, despite its greater thematic density, Arden's next play, *Live Like Pigs* (1958), is also concerned less with developing an action than defining a situation—the situation of the once-nomadic Sawney family, enmeshed at last in the charitable net of the welfare state, and compulsorily council-housed on an aspiring-to-middle-class estate. Although the tensions between the Sawneys and their respectable semi-detached neighbors, the Jacksons, reach a climax of recriminatory violence, it is impossible to give this outcome a simplistic explanation—whether as an attack on the welfare state, a defense of the rough and ready virtues of the Sawneys, or even a study in hopeless incompatibility. This is not because of any failure on Arden's part to recognize the sociopolitical implications of his work, but precisely because he is aware of the immensity and tortuousness of abstract "problems" as soon as they are rendered into individual human terms.

"The play is in large part meant to be funny," Arden notes in his preface, and the point is worth remembering: for the humor of *Live Like Pigs,* as is appropriate in a mannered comedy, lies more in a clearly rendered incongruity between different patterns of living than in the eccentricity of any single mode of behavior. It is true that the local bureaucrats who come up against the Sawneys — the minion of the housing department, the doctor, the police officer — are drawn a bit brusquely: but if they are made to represent officialdom too simply, at least their simplicity consists in a would-be benevolent bafflement, an honest sense of injury at the rebuffs offered to their polite paternalism, not in any big-brotherly archetyping on the author's part. In short, all the characters are recognizably human, though the Sawneys are rather more human than the others — big, ancient vagabonds, almost physically malformed by the cramped conveniences of their council house. But the Jacksons are by no means treated dismissively, though it is easy to be hostile to the qualities they embody — whether to the mother's cosy parlor-philosophy, the father's slightly shifty sense of his own uprightness, the daughter's depressed, depressing sexuality, or the whole family's sloughing-off of its working-class communal consciousness for the sake of good-and-pushy bourgeois respectability. Arden recognizes all these: but he senses, too, the pressures working on the Jacksons, which are more insidiously but no less damagingly disruptive than those working on the Sawneys.

The play is superficially naturalistic, but one has only to consider the sturdy-beggarly tongue in which the Sawneys speak to realize that Arden is here employing a device which was to become more familiar in his historical plays for distinguishing a way of life through its language. The difference between the spoken English of the Jacksons and the Sawneys is analogous to that between Arden's use of modern English to make immediately accessible the "medieval" dialogue of *Left-Handed Liberty,* and his conventionalized version of Scottish Chaucerian in

[11]

Armstrong's Last Goodnight—where it becomes alienating in the Brechtian sense. In the case of *Live Like Pigs,* both idioms are literary in origin, although in use on stage they suggest contrasting kinds of illiteracy. The ballads which introduce the scenes, and the occasional snatches of song within them, underline the danger of approaching the play naturalistically: yet they should, specifies Arden, "be in some way integrated into the action or else cut out." This organic purpose of song in Arden's plays is in marked contrast to the deliberately interruptive purpose it usually serves in Brecht's: balladry is best regarded as another of Arden's invented languages, the problems it poses dramatic rather than musical.

Two slighter, occasional pieces followed *Live Like Pigs.* The earlier, *When Is a Door Not a Door?* (1958), was "written for a class of student actors"—its intention to provide parts of roughly equal length for a specified number of players. Arden readily accepts and more than adequately (if sometimes unexpectedly) fulfills such journeyman commissions, enjoying them, as he enjoyed this, "as a purely technical exercise." And an audience's response to *When Is a Door Not a Door?* is likely to have the same quality of detached interest. All that happens is that an ill-fitting door in a humdrum office is taken off its hinges by two workmen, who trim and rehang it while the white-collar workers, tea ladies, and a deputation from the shop-floor filter back and forth across its threshold. An elaborate, hierarchical system of snobbery operates, of which only the two carpenters—residual craftsmen as they are—remain aloofly unaware; and the slight storm which works the play up to its climax is almost literally in a teacup. Perhaps the chief significance of this one-acter is that Arden should have considered it a worthwhile project: like his carpenters, he takes no less care over his craft when it has no pretensions to be art.

Wet Fish (1960) was Arden's second television play, and, for reasons outlined in its preface, is likely to be his last. It is much less ambitious than *Soldier, Soldier,* and was, says the author, "deliberately written in a flat and naturalistic manner"—the equation of flatness with naturalism arguable in principle, but appropriate enough to the tone of this hour-long anecdote. Its theme is "the physical progress of an ill-starred building contract" for the modernizing of an open-fronted fish shop, the elderly, well-intentioned owner of which is an old friend of the architect. The latter unfortunately delegates the seemingly straightforward job to a young female assistant, who proves incapable of coping with a series of crises on the site: and these expensive complications, and the recriminatory exchanges to which they give rise, turn out to involve Arden's old friend Krank, in his respectable daytime persona, and also to introduce Sir Harold Sweetman, destined to continue his town hall maneuvers in *The Workhouse Donkey.* The action amounts to no more than a "straight situation comedy," as Arden admits. But this is quite clearly a *television* comedy, depending, unlike *Soldier, Soldier,* on the emphases and shifting focus of the cameras. (The opening sequence, for example, defines the characters by looking over their shoulders at the drafts and doodles on their drawing boards.) The play is distinctively Arden's in its betrayal of its characters' best intentions and its openheartedness about their worst: but the two most compelling characters, the architect Gilbert Garnish and the ubiquitous Krank, seem to have wandered in from an altogether more solid and complex work.

Arden's most discussed and thematically resonant play—if not his most accomplished work—is undoubtedly *Serjeant Musgrave's Dance* (1959). It is peopled with weather-grained men and women who are no less unmistakably the playwright's own than those of *Wet Fish:* yet here the complexity is of an altogether different order. Arden's earlier works had all been more or less comic in emphasis, and set in the urban dinginess of a more or less contemporary England: and the combination in

[13]

Serjeant Musgrave's Dance of a more serious tone with an archetypally Victorian setting creates an important precedent that relates significantly to Arden's stylistic assumptions. *Musgrave* and the later *Armstrong's Last Goodnight* and *Left-Handed Liberty* are not "period" plays in the same sense as Osborne's *Luther,* or even John Whiting's *The Devils:* rather, history is here used as a kind of moral correlative—a means of making slightly unfamiliar, and so of objectifying, continuing ethical dilemmas. There is no dissembling about this intention —*Musgrave* is subtitled "an un-historical parable"—and nothing whimsical about its realization. The plays create utterly convincing worlds of truly-textured humanity—but worlds which are self-defining, and so self-contained. Rooted in a profound sense of the past—*Armstrong's Last Goodnight,* in particular, has an almost uncanny feeling of authenticity about it—Arden's history plays are nevertheless mythic rather than pedantic in their treatment of events and preoccupations: they distill from the past those elements to which the present will respond because they speak to and even anticipate its needs.

Serjeant Musgrave's Dance evolved from "three main images," according to Arden: "the big market place scene, the scene with the soldiers in the stable at night, and the soldiers' arrival in the town." It was, in the event, in inverted order that these became focal points of the action, which is completed during one evening and the next morning—the tightest time-scale Arden has ever imposed upon a full-length work. In the first act the swart, sardonic Serjeant Musgrave and three private soldiers serving under him arrive in a virtually snowbound northern town, ostensibly to conduct a recruiting campaign. But their true mission is a strange mixture of the subversive and the puritanical. Musgrave wishes to win over the townsfolk to his own austere pacifism, intending to impress them with the force of his dourly eloquent personality, and to confront the waverers with the skeleton of one of their own comrades—

whose murder in a colonial war set off the gruesome chain of reprisals which finally converted Musgrave and his colleagues to their messianic mission.

In the second act the soldiers seem to be getting their recruiting drive under way, the better to refute its deceptively convivial purposes: but that night Sparky, the youngest of them, is killed as he tries to abscond with the barmaid, Annie, from the loft in which he and his comrades are sleeping. Only in the final act do the remaining deserters reveal themselves, hoisting on a lamp-bracket in the market square not a flag but the skeleton beneath which Musgrave performs his dance of hypnotic persuasion. His mad logic of further reprisals breaks down, however, before the antagonism of the workers on whose support he had counted, and his only willing accomplice turns out to be the crippled bargee, a cunning parasite who has lurked chorically round the perimeter of the action. The townsfolk finally turn against Musgrave when Annie, nursing the skeleton that was once her sweetheart, speaks tauntingly of the death of Sparky: and with the thaw comes the imperial *deus ex machina*—a captain of dragoons, and a warrant for Musgrave's arrest.

"I think," Arden has commented, "that many of us must at some time have felt an overpowering urge to match some particularly outrageous piece of violence with an even greater and more outrageous retaliation." But instead of rationalizing such an impulse into some more civilized but probably impotent gesture, Musgrave tries to multiply-out a vengeance of his own. His failure can be interpreted equally as a condemnation of pacifism or of militarism, while the refusal of the local workers to come to his aid can be seen as either a betrayal of a fellow revolutionary or a far-sighted recognition of Musgrave's darker qualities. Indeed, the only characters in this prolifically-cast play who can be judged unequivocally are those who represent the forces of law and order, and so wear only their public faces. The play has the plausibility of such contradictions—for *what* hap-

[15]

pens matters less, in the event, than the conflicts of motive that underlie the action. And Arden's own feeling "that there is something wrong with the play" relates less to any failure in doing what it sets out to do than to its cramming in too much besides.

As Arden has recognized, the episode that is most clearly scene-setting in intention—the assembling of the soldiers in the churchyard at the close of the first act—actually withholds almost as much information as it gives out. But the play's top-heaviness is not so much in exposition as in explication, and what is lost in the blurring of the narrative line is regained dramatically in a detailed unraveling of the texture of time and place. Thus, however ambiguously the play's message may emerge, the cumulative details of Victorian working-class life compel and convince, whether in the individuality of the characters— particularly in the public-house scenes—or in the glimpses of the class system and the class struggle that emerge when bosses and workers conflict. It is a remarkable achievement that Arden should thus have enriched his soldiers' tale—indeed, have mirrored its assumptions and its power-structure at civilian level. And the characters, too, reflect one another's qualities, often ironically: the towering, erect Musgrave set against the grudging, stooped bargee; or the grimly pragmatic landlady, bearing gifts that betoken a grudging respect to the imprisoned serjeant in the final scene, set against her own brazen yet vulnerable serving-girl, Annie.

"I think a play set in the modern age," Arden has said, "should have the atmosphere of the modern age which the future historian would recognize." His own sense of history, as *Musgrave* affirms, is in just this Whig tradition: yet in approaching the present he has almost always felt it necessary to temper its immediacy by adopting a variety of comedic tones. The variety is itself suggestive of uncertainty, and *The Happy Haven* (1960) is the least formally assured of all Arden's full-length plays.

[16]

Veering between claustrophobic mannered comedy and the stylized convolutions of *commedia dell' arte* — the enacted obsessions of comedy of humours adding their own confusing flavor to the hotchpotch — *The Happy Haven* is set in the old people's home which gives it its title. The action follows the ill-fated though scrupulously clinical search of the superintendent, Dr. Copperthwaite, for an elixir of youth, which he intends to test on his own elderly patients. This intention is betrayed, however, and the rebellious inmates force their guardian to take his own medicine, the play ending as a nearly senile widow who never had the child she wanted nurses the newborn Copperthwaite on her knee.

Though the doctor's antiseptic sensibility gives rise to occasionally telling moments, as he takes the audience on the interrupted guided tour of his hospital that is the framework of the play, he is never humanized, and so does not exist in quite the same dimension as the old people. His concern for them is couched in the opening scene in a motor-mechanical jargon that exactly expresses his fascination not with individuals but with collections of invitingly decrepit moving parts. But if the plottings and jealousies of the old people are not sentimentalized, their treatment does veer awkwardly between the almost naturalistic and the caricatured as the needs of the unnecessarily busy subplots dictate. Arden specifies a "formalized presentation" for the play, which was written for an open stage: but it is doubtful how far this need for formalization is organic, and how far it is imposed by the practical necessity for the roles of energetic old people to be taken by young and consequently masked actors. Certainly, the opportunity for *commenting upon* the fact of being old that the use of masks offers is not fruitfully seized; indeed, the play thus underlines its own missed opportunities, for although "envy and impotent desire" are the prevailing passions of Arden's five pensioners as of Swift's Struldbrugs, neither the full satiric potential of their predicament nor the related truth this might tell about existing medical means of prolonging old age into senility is fully realized.

Just occasionally a sudden flash of insight into the degrees of mutual distrust, guilt, and evasion that characterize the relationship between young and old will startle one into registering the inconsequence of so much of the surrounding action. But the image of old age the play develops in such moments of clear-sighted compassion loses focus amidst heavily articulated plot-developments which are detrimental not in their density but in their sheer *separateness* from the "real" problems of aging. And since this concentration is at the cost of Arden's usually consummate sense of the particular and the local, when the play does make moral generalizations they refer back to nothing much.

The return to contextual explicitness in his next comedy, *The Workhouse Donkey* (1963), was accordingly all the more welcome. This is a raucous belly-laugh of a play—gutsy and flamboyant, yet full of unexpected nooks and crannies in its characterization. Set in an anonymous northern industrial town "somewhere between Sheffield and Leeds," the plot turns on the campaign of Alderman Charlie Butterthwaite to oust from office the newly appointed Chief Constable, Colonel Feng, whose zealous probings into laws riddled with time-honored loopholes have seemingly aligned him with the Conservative opposition in the council chamber, led by the brewing magnate Sir Harold Sweetman. For the Labour Party—in control of the council for some three decades, and thus in effect the local establishment—though undeniably doing its best for the town, has sometimes, on the side, done a little too much for its own leading members.

Such municipal "corruption"—of an insignificance symbolized by the round of after-hours drinks for the councilors that first lands them in trouble with Feng—does not seem too promising raw material for a comedy as raucous and Aristophanic in intention as *The Workhouse Donkey*. And even the slightly dirtier linen that goes through the political mangle as the conflict

[18]

proceeds—Sweetman's share in the running of a disreputable strip-club, a mass foreclosure on Butterthwaite's gambling debts that tempts him into robbing the town-hall safe—seems less the stuff of which good plays are made than grubby elections lost. Yet it is because such incidents are so closely rooted in day-to-day politicking—indeed, they are only the breadth of a libel-writ away from actual incidents, amalgamated and rearranged —that their overflowing into the play's set pieces of ribaldry becomes a matter not of the converging coincidences of farce but of evoking the remedial laughter of true comedy. Butterthwaite's final gesture of defiance before his defeat is thus to organize a march of the lowlier workers from whom his strength derives upon Sweetman's newly opened art gallery: and by this he measures the distance between his own breeding and outlook—once the "workhouse donkey" of the title, now determined to better the lot of his fellow outcasts—and the mandarin self-interest of the brewing magnates and their kind.

There are other Arden archetypes in the play besides Butterthwaite—Wellington Blomax, for example, financial *éminence grise* and unorthodox medical adviser to the Labour group, who is a slightly more respectable version of Krank, his amorality tempered by perverse notions of principle, and Colonel Feng, recognizably cast in the same rigid mold as Musgrave. Thus, the colonel's stern morality is vitiated by its very intractability, and even his speech habits are reminiscent of the serjeant's:

I am a man under authority. Having soldiers under me, or at least constables, and I say to this man "go" and he goeth, and to another "come" and he cometh, and to my servant "do this" and he doeth it.

After which Feng bursts into a blank-verse reflection upon his dilemma:

> Not difficult to prevail but difficult indeed
> To live and hold that prevalence, yet live
> A social and communicating creature.

[19]

> The law by nature is civilian,
> But it can only work through mode of warfare.

he restrictive verse straitjacket here serves to emphasize the ersonal and social hemming-in to which Feng's office subjects iim; it is used again for Sweetman's statement of his ethic and ambition, though here in a more measured manner:

> My three tall sons
> Inhabit or have inhabited public schools.
> They grow to love the world I set them in,
> And, loving it, become it as they walk.
> I am a prince, I am a baron, sirs!
> And yet I have no sovereignty, no.
> For what is power of gold when politics
> At every turn deny my high aspiring?
> The election lights on Butterthwaite.

And the bathos is as calculated as the harsher rhythms of the collective northern thumbing-of-the-nose that is the play's epilogue and, in effect, its moral:

> Withdraw those quivering nostrils
> We smell as we think decent
> If we tell you we've cleaned our armpits
> You'd best believe we've cleaned 'em recent.
> We have washed them white and whiter
> Than the whitewash on the wall
> And if for THE WORKHOUSE DONKEY
> We should let one tear down fall
> Don't think that he's coming back . . .
> The old sod's gone for good and all!

It is in one sense misleading, of course, to cite only these contrasting kinds of poetic apologia: but it is precisely because Arden employs them for a direct, explicatory purpose that the critic finds himself quoting from passages of verse rather than the prose in which the action is *carried forward,* as distinct from commented upon. And *The Workhouse Donkey* is, as the epilogue explains, an invitation to take it or leave it — this warts-and-all way of life in the millrace of the mixed economy.

[20]

Of course, there are Arden's usual comic complications of plot, which trick out the play to three substantial acts: and the author's preface even suggests that he could have wished it longer—"six or seven or thirteen hours," maybe, during which the audience could come and go at will, assisted by a printed synopsis of the action. Arden was to return to this concept of "promenade playgoing" in *The Hero Rises Up*—though again failing to reconcile his theoretic ideal with an audience's customary expectations. Nevertheless, a certain irrelevance is as much at the core of *The Workhouse Donkey* as an undoubted irreverence. Take the gratuitous striptease in Sweetman's club; or the non-starter of a romance between a self-doubting Feng and Blomax's daughter; or the instant committee-meetings which materialize whenever two or three councilors are gathered together; or the unexpected liaison between a lugubrious police sergeant and the club hostess: without these and all the rest of its extraneous events, the play would be tidier and more controllable—but it would also have lost much of its heart.

Though Arden's reworking of the Christmas story into *The Business of Good Government* dates from 1960, and thus strictly precedes *The Workhouse Donkey* (just as its title ironically anticipates the theme of the later play), it is probably more helpful to regard it as a tentative exploration of the territory the dramatist was to explore more fully in *Ironhand, Armstrong's Last Goodnight,* and *Left-Handed Liberty.* For if *The Workhouse Donkey* is a wildly inventive contemporary extravaganza, the politics of the other plays are, like those of the nativity piece, at once more sober and—as seriousness almost invariably implies in Arden's work—a matter of history. Not that "seriousness" is to be equated with solemnity: simply, there is not the same need —when time lends a distance of its own—that Arden's broader style of humor should set the action back a further pace. But the dilemma faced by his pragmatic Herod in *The Business of Good Government* is that of any moderately well-intentioned politician

[21]

confronted with the certain perils and uncertain advantages of any revolutionary force:

Goodwill, great joy, peace upon earth—I do not believe they are altogether possible. But it is the business of good government to try and make them possible.

Herod is outwardly much as the Old Wise Man describes him— "a man of high intelligence, genuinely understanding the responsibilities of power and with an enlightened attitude towards philosophy and science." But these responsibilities require him to order the massacre of the innocents—and thus ensure, as he realizes, his own eternal shame. "It is fitting," he believes, "that the honor of one man should die for the good of the people." Yet in the event it is not, of course, so much Herod's honor as the good of the people that is in dispute.

The play was designed for amateur performance in a west country parish church, and served this original purpose well. It retains added interest as Arden's first attempt at a kind of community drama that has since preoccupied him: and as a printed script it fails only in disappointing the expectations it arouses of a fuller development of Herod's character—for the emphasis shifts, and the action is rather perfunctorily rounded off as soon as the flight into Egypt is accomplished. The play also digresses colorfully into the bureaucratic business of the tax-gathering in Bethlehem, contrasting the reactions to it of the baffled but resigned shepherds, the put-upon hostess of the inn, and a travel-worn but phlegmatic Joseph. And it is probably this carpenter's advice to the shepherds after they have visited the infant Jesus that comes closest to a direct statement of the play's philosophy:

All these things will be known in good time. Here is the baby: here is his mother .   .   .   your sheep are left out on the hills. You had better go back now and look after them. If it was a good dream: then you will dream it again one day. If it wasn't—well, the world has to carry on turning. There are trees must be cut down and the timber to be shaped, there are houses to need roofs, the ships to need their frames, there are always the cradles will need to be rocked. And each one of these works will call for its true attention . . . . Thank you for coming.

It is a notable achievement that Arden can counterpoint the immediacy of such practical considerations—whether these arise from Herod's national interests or Joseph's pressing order book—with his spiritual theme. And if it is arguable that this theme is understated—or rather, treated too much as one of the "givens" of the situation—this is perhaps because the whole play resembles more an episode from a modern mystery cycle than a self-contained work, both in its unself-conscious blending of the archaic with the contemporary and, less successfully, in the feeling of jaggedness about a resolution that resolves an incident rather than an action.

Arden has himself described his adaptation of Goethe's *Goetz von Berlichingen* into *Ironhand* (1961) as "a workshop piece," which he has since used as source material for *Armstrong*, and to a lesser extent for *Left-Handed Liberty*. It is characteristic of his sheer professionalism that he should thus be prepared to write off as a technical exercise what amounts to a substantial and in some sense original piece of work. But it is true that the importance of the play does lie more in the belated justice it does to Goethe than in Arden's own contribution, which consists mainly in a hardening of the role of Weislingen into a more worthy antagonist for Goetz, an unequivocal identification of Goethe's Brother Martin with Luther, and a tightening up of certain expository and structural weaknesses. The conflict between romantic but often reactionary individualism and the notion of liberal but perhaps stultifying civil order is persuasively embodied in the characters of Goetz and Weislingen, and the latter's agonizings are those of the humanist in any age who becomes aware of the discrepancy between his aims and the means available for their realization:

I am the instrument of the law, sir, not its creator.   .   .   .   I ask myself this: what will be the effect of all these executions upon the young men who have to carry them out? I am afraid they may come to take pleasure in their work: and then what will happen? But with the help of God, order and peace will be here before that.

And Goetz dies dreaming of

Freedom. And no warfare. Freedom. And good order. Freedom.

As in *The Business of Good Government*, it is the problem (perhaps the impossibility) of reconciling liberty and order, freedom and justice, that is very much at the center of *Ironhand*, as it was to be of the two historical plays that followed it.

Thus, it is not sufficient to say, as does John Russell Taylor, that Goetz is merely an anachronism, "a man who belongs to the Middle Ages, and does not understand that the historical processes at work around him in Germany make him obsolete." For while Arden is indeed almost unique among his contemporaries in his ability to dramatize such abstractions as "historical processes," he is able to do so precisely because he *humanizes* them: and the living creatures he creates, like those twentieth-century anachronisms the Sawneys in *Live Like Pigs*, remain, awkwardly but indisputably, as physically *there* as Charlie Butterthwaite—or, more to the present point, as that "great bull . . . of a man," the title character of *Armstrong's Last Goodnight* (1964). This play had its beginnings in Arden's overlapping reading of the medieval Scottish "Ballad of Johnny Armstrong" and the book on the then still turbulent Congo situation by Conor Cruise O'Brien, *To Katanga and Back*. He was immediately struck by the similarities between

Sir David Lindsay, this civilized poet and conventional diplomat sent out by James V to deal with a violent situation in the tribal part of Scotland, and O'Brien, brought up among all the trappings of a civilized society, accustomed to the ways of European statecraft, a man of letters. He, too, was sent out where diplomacy had to do with murder and threats of murder. This parallel mustn't be pressed too far, but in both cases one

[24]

sees the opposition of two opposed kinds of received values, the impact of one upon the other.

In transposing the Congolese problem into mid-sixteenth-century Scotland Arden was not, he emphasizes, attempting a *roman à clef:* for the similarities between Lindsay's and O'Brien's situations were not political or economic, let alone racial, but moral. The questions confronting both were of political expediency — its virtues and, more particularly, its limitations.

Lindsay, court poet and influential tutor to the boy king James, wishes to bring civil order to Scotland, and ensure peace with England, by quelling the depredations of the border raider Johnny Armstrong. By bribery and betrayal he avoids shedding blood other than Armstrong's own: but in so doing he sacrifices not only his own integrity but the life of a man whose loyalty was there for the winning. For Armstrong, though anarchically independent, is ungrudging in his friendships — and naïvely susceptible to his sovereign's flattery. He exults that "the king hath callit me brither," only to realize that his promised safe-conduct is not to the court but the gallows.

Thus outlined, the plot is simple, and seemingly in a tradition of medieval romanticism sustained not so much by the Middle Ages as by Sir Walter Scott. Yet the *tone* of the play instantly qualifies such an impression. Armstrong's instincts are all as primitive as his loyalties — his cruelty, when aroused, as uncompromising — and he is capable of being overwhelmed by even the most trivial trappings of "civilization." His clansmen inhabit another world from that of the polished commissioners: and these peripheral characters contribute to an antithesis that works both visually — in the contrast between Armstrong's tough, naturally aristocratic tribe and the bland, begowned diplomats, for instance — and verbally, in the different habits of mind that can be discerned in the distance between the Armstrongs' brief, broadly functional utterances and the measured, sophisticated cadences of the court. Both are variations upon Arden's ersatz

[25]

version of medieval Scottish—indebted to the literary language, and closely rooted in the balladry that knits the play together, but essentially a stage convention of a dialect, alien yet recognizable. It achieves, nevertheless, an often poetic precision—as here, in Lindsay's epilogue to the play, which anticipates the legend concerning Armstrong's gallows tree:

> It did fail and it did wither upon the hill of Carlanrigg, as ane dry exemplar to the warld: here may ye read the varieties of dishonour, and determine in your mind how best ye can avoid whilk ane of them, and when. Remember: King James the Fift, though but seventeen years of age, did become ane adult man, and learnt to rule his kingdom. He had been weel instructit in the necessities of state by that poet that was his tutor.

This idiom—as the occasional infiltrations of Gaelic remind an audience—is intended only to inflict slight shocks of non-recognition: to serve as an unobtrusive but continuous reminder of the fact that these events are taking place in a foreign country—as Scotland was—and of their historical period. The theme of *Left-Handed Liberty*, for example, was to make it much less necessary that either should be emphasized.

The play is, in short, much more medieval than it is romantic. Even for its staging, Arden suggests a modification of the "simultaneous mansions" convention: Armstrong's castle at stage right, James's palace at stage left, with a single tree up center representing the wild lands of the border. The fluidity of the play's movement is thus increased—appropriately, for its action amounts much more to an unfolding explication of *character* than is usual in Arden's work, which tends to employ an episodic structure to focus attention on the interaction of *events*. There are, it is true, some subtle political machinations to be sorted out: but these are not so much significant in themselves as manifestations of Lindsay's diplomatic persona, in which he attempts to play off this lord against that, one religion against another—and, in his own mind, principle against expediency.

[26]

And through my craft and my humanity
I will save the realm frae butchery
Gif I can, good sir, but gif I can.

If Armstrong's death has been brought about by Lindsay's treachery, the borderer has, however, been guilty of just the same combination of craft and butchery in the murder of Wamphrey at the beginning of the play: like Lindsay, moreover, he engineers but is not personally implicated in his crime. And the stabbing of McGlass, Lindsay's secretary, makes a third violent death enacted on stage. This, and the half-crazed mourning of Meg, Wamphrey's mistress; the itinerant sermonizing of the Evangelist; the precocious, secondhand wisdom of the fragile king; the brutish intrusions of the squat Gaelic-speaking Highlanders; even the contrast between Armstrong's quiet and chaste wife and Lindsay's mistress, compulsive in a sensuality that captivates his antagonist besides—all contribute to the rich fabric of the play, against which the relationship of Lindsay and Armstrong moves toward its resolution.

But it is perhaps necessary to insist that this relationship is *all* that is resolved. "The man is deid," Lindsay sums up, "there will be no war with England: this year." *This year:* such is the limit of his political achievement. And it has cost him his soul—as a Christian, the damnation he has earlier prophesied to McGlass. Not that Arden is overassertive about Lindsay's failures, political or personal; he allows the "alarming and hateful events" to speak for themselves. But elsewhere he has insisted:

My views on the Armstrong story are positive enough—Lindsay was wrong. But as to what he should have done to avoid self-destruction: there is a question that I cannot pretend to answer. The whole of life is a series of such cruxes.

And, asked by a lady journalist at the time of *Armstrong's* first production if he were ever going to write a play which did offer a solution to the problem of violence, Arden replied:

There is no solution, except not to practice violence. I don't think she thought this was a very good answer: but in all humility, it is no worse than the answers given by Christ to similar questions. His method was usually to tell an illustrative anecdote. I believe this is also the method of the theatre.

This idea of a play as an exemplary parable which is nevertheless inexplicit, or at least open-ended, is no longer entirely acceptable to Arden — nor, for that matter, is the principle of nonviolence. But both are central to an understanding of *Armstrong's Last Goodnight*.

Typically, Arden takes care to set out his historical credentials — and where he has chosen to abandon authenticity for the sake of dramatic convenience — in the prefaces both to *Armstrong's Last Goodnight* and to his next full-length play, *Left-Handed Liberty* (1965). But though he had found it possible in *Armstrong* not only to shape the substance of history but also to capture the tenor and texture of a period, it is, as Arden confesses, more difficult "to know exactly what thirteenth century statesmen and clerics were thinking about." Accordingly, *Left-Handed Liberty*, while retaining the form of a prose epic chronicle, also becomes an exploration of historical methodology, championing what Herbert Butterfield described disparagingly as the Whig interpretation of history: the description and evaluation of the past not on its own terms but according to present-day values and present-day needs.

Underrated and relatively seldom performed though it is, I believe *Left-Handed Liberty* succeeds, and does so not least in its recognition and turning to account of its own limitations. Its theme has no such point of tangential reference in contemporary events as *Musgrave* or *Armstrong*, but was the result of a commission for Arden from the City of London for a work to commemorate the 750th anniversary of the signing of Magna Carta. And its language, while achieving an appropriate colloquial robustness, made no such attempt to find an acceptable means of rendering its own archaic quality as did that of *Armstrong*. Indeed, if the idiom of that previous play had grown out of its own use of balladry, *Left-Handed Liberty* is the more completely a prose work, the punctuating purpose of its verse passages more reminiscent of their use in *Musgrave*. But in other respects *Left-Handed Liberty* takes Arden's historical method to its logical extreme. In beginning rather than ending his play with the signing of Magna Carta, Arden sets out to show the ineffectiveness of a document drawn up as a political compromise which neither side intended to respect, but which has been hewn into a cornerstone of English liberty by later historical accidents. And in charting the unhappy but ultimately inconsequential struggle for supremacy which continued after the signing of the charter until John's death, he relishes at last the ironic irrelevance of that death itself—"my frantic history," as John laconically comments, "suspended under circumstances of absolute uncertainty."

Now inconsequence is no easy subject-matter for a play as completely divorced from the formal premises of Theatre of the Absurd as *Left-Handed Liberty*: nor is inconclusiveness, by definition, an easy conclusion. Indeed, both John himself, and the omnipresent Papal Legate, Pandulph, are well aware of this, inhabiting, as they do, twin streams of temporal consciousness which converge at the play's moments of stepping outside itself:

The liberation of Norfolk, completed in mid-October, 1216, is an item of military history of no great consequence whatever. So off you go— get on with it.

Thus John's long third-act soliloquy to the audience—an overlapping justification of his existence as a historical fact and as a character in a play—is the necessary rounding-off to the action conceived as Whig historical overview, just as the vividly mimed but ultimately bathetic wading through the wrongly predicted tide of the Wash draws its line beneath the "dramatic" action. But this duality is in no sense Pirandellian, for although John's tongue-in-cheek tramping from one level of action to the other is entirely convincing, the duality has to do not with "illusion and reality" but with two realities separated by seven centuries—and, curiously, Arden succeeds in affirming and even vindicating both.

Ultimately, *what* is vindicated is not an act of political expediency or its idealization by later generations, let alone one side of the struggle in its contemporary trappings, but everyman's essential fallibility. John sums up in his soliloquy:

Inconsistent, irregular, unreasonable. And this is our uniqueness. Not in our capacity for damnation or salvation nor yet in our capacity for logical rationality—though both of them are glorious: and both of them, I fear, have distorted our nature.

Certainly, one senses an unusual degree of sympathy on Arden's part for the king who thus celebrates variegated humanity—"that almost Oriental monster of your history books," as Pandulph describes him, whose household records nevertheless "show him to have been a tireless administrator, devoted to the pursuit of justice." And it is surely in demonstration of John's belief in the "inconsistent, irregular, unreasonable," that some of the play's liveliest scenes—the barons romping with their whores, John's dispensing of Azdak-like justice through his southern counties, a splendid afterthought of a scene written when Arden "remembered the legend of the Wise Men of Gotham and regretted that I failed to insert it in my story"—are, strictly speaking, irrelevant to the action. For the play makes clear at its outset that, judged in the light of history, the main action itself is irrelevant. What is extraneous, whether in the sprawling set-piece scenes or the subtle undercurrents of conflict between personalities, is precisely what gives the play its flavor. And the confrontations between characters of widely differing political or moral philosophies become the more revealing in their isolation from heavily illustrative purposes.

Thus, the loyal Marshal whose integrity John is quite prepared to betray for his own devious ends is set against his rebel son, clinging to the ideals of a chivalrous code he has in practice abandoned. The stolid, pragmatically peaceful Lord Mayor offers refuge to barons who actively despise his own bourgeois beliefs and mode of living. The gaunt, eerily erect figure of John's mother in the first scene, waspishly critical of her son's weaknesses even as she prepares to die, continues to haunt the king's motives, only half-exorcised by the less scrupulous bearing and sensuously alert responses of his mistress, the Lady de Vesci. The self-torturing Archbishop Langton, his loyalties divided three ways between a weak but truly ordained king, a catholic church incapable of grasping the realities of a situation a continent away, and the irreligious barons for whom he has drafted the terms of the charter, veers unhappily between mediation and mere compromise. And the pervasive Pandulph upholds against all comers—the audience included—the rigid degrees and priorities of medievalism. Only the barons seem at first to fit less easily into the play's dialectic structure—for most of their thinking is done for them: but they are essential to the more strikingly dramatic functioning of the action, their brute force impinging upon it the more terrifyingly for the civilized veneer the "thinking" characters usually manage to preserve.

Left-Handed Liberty is, as I write, Arden's most recent major work for the stage: and a discussion of the plays he has written in the seven years since its performance—as of one or two earlier works so far passed over—will demand rather different critical terms of reference. Of these, three—*Ars Longa, Vita Brevis, Friday's Hiding,* and *The Royal Pardon*—are "community dramas," intended as scenarios for elaboration rather than definitive texts. Two—*The Hero Rises Up,* and an as yet unperformed work about the Irish situation—are "romantic melodramas." One, *The Bagman,* is an autobiographical allegory for radio. Another, *Harold Muggins Is a Martyr,* is an agitprop

[31]

extravaganza which has been performed but not published. And only *The True History of Squire Jonathan and His Unfortunate Treasure* (1963) falls within a more conventional dramatic genre, albeit one previously little explored by Arden — that of the anecdotal one-act play.

The collective publication of *Squire Jonathan* with *The Bagman* as *Two Autobiographical Plays* came some eight years after the composition of the earlier play, and eighteen after its inspiration in an abortive love affair: but there seems only a tenuous link between the "Grimm fairy-tale Gothic" of its castellated setting and the forthrightness of Arden's prefatory recollection of his lost Scottish love. Hence the metamorphosis of a raw student of architecture, calling himself a poet to his girl friend's dismay, into the stunted hero of Arden's play — the hereditary and vaguely medieval Squire Jonathan, impregnable and alone,

with a body as cadaverous as it is hairy, with ribs like prongs of a garden fork, a navel like an egg-cup full of dust, a ridiculously wrinkled pair of cullions, and a well-loved drooping yard that very badly desires employment.

To solve this unemployment problem arrives the "great blonde milky woman" of Squire Jonathan's dreams — who is duly pampered and petted and decorated with the treasures of a miser's lifetime, until she is walking around the tower "like a huge embellished elephant." Jonathan's language is full of such luxurious simile: the woman is elsewhere a "lurching hay-cart," a "vast unfolded circus-tent all a-flap and a-jingle in the buffet of the wind." Yet much of it has the compensatory quality of an image lingered over in lonely introspection, rather than created in a sudden fusion of activity and imagination. Jonathan has a brooding fixation, too, about the charcoal-burners in the nearby forest, who occasionally taunt him and who will, he fears, eventually abduct his great milky woman, not much against her will. And, sure enough — the suspicions themselves turning her friendship sour—the visitor unpicks her chastity belt with the pin of one of Jonathan's costly brooches, and leaps naked from the window into the arms of the dark men of the forest lurking beneath.

As the first play on a British stage thus to employ such mobile nudity, *Squire Jonathan* achieved a certain notoriety, yet its point—as of a similarly unteasing strip in *Harold Muggins*—lay precisely in its ordinariness. "Now, here I am," as the woman remarks. "With what do you propose to cover me, instead?" But the pitiable Jonathan, for all his fine dreams, can cover his woman only with his own shame, and so loses her. The play is pleasantly anecdotal, fitting appropriately into a playing time of about forty minutes, and it is memorable for linguistic flourishes as self-consciously Gothic as its setting: like so much of Arden's less ambitious work, it has no pretensions to be more than it is —a recollection distorted in tranquillity by an author who "no longer bore anybody malice."

Squire Jonathan and *The Bagman* are exceptional among Arden's later plays in lacking a collaborative title-page credit to his wife, the actress Margaretta D'Arcy. But although Miss D'Arcy had earlier had a share in the writing of *The Business of Good Government,* the extent and nature of the Ardens' collaboration remains conjectural. And it may or may not be significant that the two of his more recent works for which Arden asserts sole responsibility should also be those open to a more or less orthodox critical approach—unlike, say, *Ars Longa, Vita Brevis* (1963), which was originally commissioned for a series of children's plays, and was also performed professionally during Peter Brook's Theatre of Cruelty season in 1964. The play's half-a-dozen episodes, even shorter in sum than *Squire Jonathan,* seem to have been selected more for their theatrical effectiveness than for any particular expository purpose: they illustrate the arrival of a new art master at a tinpot private school, where his ruthless expunging of any aesthetic activity more sensuous than the drawing of straight lines and geometric patterns eventually attracts him toward the equally rigorous disciplines of the territorial army. Disguised in the course of his military duties as a tree, he is shot, not altogether accidentally, by the headmaster, who raises a fund for a widow more than a little relieved by the opportunity to leave her husband's straight and narrow.

This *Musgrave* of the schoolmaster's common room works both as a snippet of absurdist insight and as a kind of concise coda to Arden's work so far. As Theatre of the Absurd—or the closest Arden has ever come to exploring its potential—the play veers between scrupulously overgrammatical awkwardness and a stream of revelatory half-consciousness that is reminiscent of Ionesco's early work. Here is one such verbally glutted moment from the headmaster's speech-day oration:

An appreciation of art is very important these days if we want our children to be accepted upon equal terms in the wide world of business politics technology housewifery orthography archaeology psephology pseudo-psephology ecclesiology and the organization of bingo. We must move with the times.

And here, at the other extreme, is the art master, shocked into lucidity by headmasterly disapproval of the rather serious wargame into which his advocacy of ruthless discipline has plunged an unsuspecting class:

I fear I have so aggravated the headmaster that I must lose my employment unless he have a change of mind before tomorrow. Is this not enough for you, that you should withhold from me my tea into the bargain?

Certainly, one can understand the attraction of *Ars Longa* as an acting exercise, demanding, as it does, so many similar stylistic transitions within its brief bounds. But Arden stresses that he prefers a less agonized approach to his text:

When we . . . directed the play ourselves with the Kirbymoorside Girl Guides we threw out all the dialogue, except two bits of verse, and let them improvise their own words throughout. The result, was, we thought, much more successful than any of the productions we have seen where my dialogue was adhered to by the cast.

Surely no dramatist other than Arden could thus write a play simultaneously to satisfy the requirements of the Royal Shakespeare Company in its most experimental mood and the Kirbymoorside Girl Guides.

It was a natural enough extension of this attitude that in their next collaborative work, *Friday's Hiding* (1965), Arden and Margaretta D'Arcy should use very few words at all. The play's title refers to Farmer Balfour's ritual evasion of his two underpaid farm-laborers and a housekeeper-sister after his weekly visit to the bank: and the consequences of the enraged farmhands' imagined murder of their employer are mimed against the day-to-day abrasiveness of the master-servant relationship. The play's dialect stage-directions in free verse constitute rather more than nine-tenths of its printed script — making the work impressionistically a curious combination of *The Playboy of the Western World* and Peter Handke's *My Foot My Tutor*. But the relative emphases are for the actors to discover. "Not being by temperament as definitive as, say, Mr. Beckett," the Ardens note, they preferred telling a story in their stage directions — indicating "by variations in the typography the different stages of the narrative and the relative rhythms of the action" — to setting out precisely choreographed instructions. But although permitting this degree of freedom, the authors insist upon the essential accuracy of the way of life they portray. "It would," they claim, "be a serious error for the actors playing Mr. and Miss Balfour to portray the one as a miserable old skinflint and the other as a dried-up sour spinster."

They should much rather be the rosy-cheeked bright-eyed toytown figures out of a child's picture-book of the countryside, and let the opposite elements in their personalities arise through the action.

The play is in sum "an ironic statement—*not* an affirmation—of the deep-rootedness of conservative values." It is also very funny: yet its humor stems not from the grossness of baldly mimetic actions but from the clear recognition of a way of life which has been temporarily tilted off-balance.

The Royal Pardon (1966) came as a natural though not altogether satisfactory culmination to what might be called the rural rather than the urban aspect of the Ardens' work in the field of "community drama." The earlier playlets had been closely rooted in the particular societies or conditions from which they sprang, which happened to be of the countryside. They were evocative rather than overtly critical in manner, and more or less found their own appropriate brevity. In stretching itself to full-length, and to some extent losing touch with its own kind of pastoral particularity, *The Royal Pardon* succeeds as a good quality children's play of a conventionally "mythic" kind. An authorial note confirms that "the period is legendary rather than historical"—and the sense of community is equally vague. A company of strolling players, hounded as rogues and vagabonds by a traditional village constable, is joined—and rejuvenated—by a deserting soldier called Luke. The actors obtain not only their eponymous pardon from the King of England but his authority to perform at the French court, where they win the King of France's prize of a hundred guineas for a hastily improvised play in which everything goes wrong for the best. The down-at-heel pride of the players is as exactly caught as their half-cocked histrionics, the wary relationship between stage and state is nicely barbed, and the succession of sudden reversals and rewards is well calculated for a childish audience. But although the action is ostensibly more ambitious than that of *Good Government* or *Ars Longa,* the total impression is confusing—the anarchy muted and almost decorous.

The script as it stands was developed in rehearsal for a shoestring arts festival at Beaford, Devon, in 1966—and thus once more conceived for and by a regional community which felt a degree of corporate identity. Arden's two entertainments for metropolitan performance were less successful in identifying their audience, and so in meeting—let alone challenging—its expectations: yet their very different failures were on an overweeningly more ambitious scale. Written in collaboration with Margaretta D'Arcy, they were *Harold Muggins Is a Martyr*, presented at the amateur, left-wing Unity Theatre Club during the summer of 1969 but never published, and *The Hero Rises Up*, staged briefly in the converted engine-shed in Chalk Farm that was once the center of Arnold Wesker's Centre Fortytwo, the Round House.

The action of *Muggins* evolved during its rehearsal period, and was strongly influenced by the ideas and peformance style of an agit-propagandist fringe group called the Cartoon Archetypical Slogan Theatre, from which the play was largely cast. What emerged was a rambling tale of a café proprietor caught between rival protection rackets—Harold Muggins, prone to exploit his handful of employees, and himself egged on by the petty ambitions of a traditional nagging wife. An Everyman figure with some incidental characteristics of the then prime minister, Harold Wilson, Muggins has a capacity for original sin that is sustained and enlarged by the corruptive and manipulative pressures of his society. Set-pieces in Arden's more strident rhyme-patterns—Muggins himself in self-pitying soliloquy, or the gangster boss Mr. Big on his organic role in society—merge into mock-heroic tableaux, episodes of writhing caricature, downbeat scenes of domestic crisis, or table-smashing punch-ups. The combination of Arden's linguistic discipline with the tortuous, harsh-tempered physical expertise of his actors was unexpected, and often irresistible.

And yet, in the most politically committed play to which he had turned his hand, Arden managed to puzzle his audience more than ever. Was *Muggins* no more than a rejection of values simplistically symbolized by formica-topped tables, brunchburgers, and neon lighting—a Cobbettian indictment of an even greater Wen? Was it a deceptively simple, actually elaborate political parable, its lampooning intentions blunted by a grudging sympathy for its put-upon hero? Certainly, it seemed typical of an earlier Arden in its refusal to take sides, rounding off even its flattest characters with ifs-and-buts of motivation: was, then, the blunt-instrumental *style* of the production inappropriate to a play which needed to hint at complexity as well as to make propaganda? Was it, in that case, *good* propaganda, if the audience's response to it was so complicated? Or was this simply a first experiment in urban community drama which had lost its way in the process of collaborative and sometimes argumentative creation?

The critics patronizingly accused the play of being patronizing. Presumably, they had gone in expectation of a cerebral crossword-puzzle, and found themselves bewildered amidst the conventions of the comic-strip. *Harold Muggins* was an offensive enough title to oversophisticated ears, and these were to be bludgeoned further by a villain called Mr. Big, a henchman called Jakey Jasper, and a crooked lawyer called Buzzard. The discussions after each performance went on for hours: but the argumentative audiences were drawn from the readers of the political weeklies, not the blocks of council houses surrounding the theatre.

Precisely what kind of community Arden hoped to tap at the Round House for *The Hero Rises Up* was never clear: but, thanks to the preface to its printed text, one is left in less doubt about the impression he hoped the play would make:

We hoped to write a play which need not be *done properly*. That is to say: we wanted to produce it ourselves so that it would present the audience with an experience akin to that of running up in a crowded wet street on Saturday night against a drunken red-nosed man with a hump on his back dancing in a puddle, his arms around a pair of

bright-eyed laughing girls, his mouth full of inexplicable loud noises.
. . . You don't at once forget him: and although you know nothing
about him, he has become a sort of circumstance in your life. You can't
sit down and analyze him, because you haven't got the needful data.
You can't ask him for his "symbolism"—if he has any, you yourself will
have provided it: and you can't go back and "re-evaluate" him, because
the police will have moved him on. But there he was: and you saw him.

One notes the assumption that *The Hero* should be *experienced*—that its action should constitute a "circumstance" rather
than a development. Now *Muggins* might conceivably have ful-
filled such an expectation—as, in good hands, might *Ars Longa.*
But *The Hero Rises Up* is much more recognizably a successor
to *Armstrong's Last Goodnight,* crossbred with *The Workhouse
Donkey.* It progresses in loosely linked episodes from Nelson's
inglorious reconquest of Naples to his legendary death at
Trafalgar, deriving a unity of sorts from its counterpointing of
political actions with the personal and social effects of its hero's
ill-concealed love affair with Emma Hamilton.

In form, the work is perhaps more a ballad play, in direct
descent from *The Beggar's Opera,* than the romantic melodrama
it proclaims itself. It even shares some of the traditional airs
used by Gay, drawing upon sea shanties and familiar folk songs
besides—the lyrics demanding a belted-out Brechtian astrin-
gency rather than careful orchestration. But one must qualify
the *interruptive* implications of that Brechtian analogy, and
again assert the *organic* function of Arden's own ballad-monger-
ing. The switching between prose and verse is a modulating
device, which creates the kind of extra dimension of time and
attitude that enables Emma not to prophesy but to *know* before
the Battle of Trafalgar:

> It's into them he will thrust his courage
> Till they toss their limbs and squeal—
> Oh sure he is worth his freestone pillar
> At the north end of Whitehall—

Four huge lions made of bronze and a great wide open square of nothing. That's for me: nothing.

Arden allows directors to fit their own tunes to the more freely-flowing lyrics, such as this: but, he notes, "there are a few songs in the text which were written to fit extant airs, and if they are not sung to those airs something of our dramatic intentions will be lost." There are, in fact, ten such songs, and they tend to be the celebratory ones—those which counterpoint a moment in the action instead of continuing it.

From an audience, *The Hero* requires concentration and a degree of detachment—and the detachment is facilitated by the doubling of certain characters as narrators and by signboard scene-captions. From a director, it demands the fashioning of grotesques from a Gilray cartoon into figures who recognizably embody certain ethical or political standpoints. Thus, Nelson—"the last uncontested hero-figure in our own history"—is projected as a Nietzschean superman to be cut cruelly down to size, the brutality of his victories brought out as clearly as the banality of his strategy: perversely, he achieves a kind of dignity only between his illicit sheets. In the last analysis, however, *The Hero,* assertive in its latter-day chapbook style, is less fruitfully ambiguous than that earlier piece of equivocal pacifist propaganda, *Serjeant Musgrave's Dance.* If Musgrave was a puritanical pacifist who compromised his gospel by staining it with blood, this Nelson is a vulgar little sailor who personifies the vanity and cruelty of his militaristic society, and who is redeemed in death only in so far as a grateful nation is revealed to be more hypocritical than himself.

The Hero Rises Up is not, then, really a "community drama" at all—at least, not in the sense in which the Ardens originally conceived the form—though in production it was perhaps the attempt to *impose* the play upon an amorphous urban community that doomed it to fail, whereas a more orthodox and professional production might, on an admittedly limited scale, have

[40]

succeeded. *Why* Arden was not prepared to work within such limitations becomes clearer—as does much else relating to his recent work—from *The Bagman; or, The Impromptu of Muswell Hill* (1969), a dream play for radio. In a sense, it is already out of date, for Arden's feelings about the uses of violence and the artist's involvement in political activity underwent a drastic change following a lengthy visit to India: and he now regards the attitude of the central character—his own persona—at the end of *The Bagman* as "reprehensible, cowardly, and not to be imitated." In spite of this, he decided to publish the text as representative of his feelings at the time, adding that it would "be better to demonstrate my opinions of 1971 in a new play—which is not yet written." So *The Bagman* serves, for the moment, as Arden's provisional taking-stock of his own achievements.

The play has something of the dreamlike texture of a dramatized *Alice in Wonderland,* and its feeling for the *acceptable* telescoping of times and places is consummate. But it is infused, too, with the concealed contemporaneity of a *Gulliver's Travels* —its surreal clarity of vision through the dark glasses of dream greatly enhanced by the nature of its intended medium, from which it would not readily adapt to the visual demands of stage performance. Arden himself is the Narrator, whose recollections bind together the blurred edges of the play's dream transitions. Searching in vain for an evening newspaper on early closing day in Muswell Hill, he is persuaded to buy an ex-army kitbag from an old woman in the park, who tells him that it just might contain an "elegant soft young woman" for his private delectation. Half aware that he is dreaming, he is chased from his bench by a keeper who suspects him of harboring objects and desires forbidden in the bylaws, and finds himself not back in the Muswell Hill Road but on a bleak moorland where half-starved women keep carrionlike watch over a decaying corpse.

Rescued from their clutches by a band of soldiers, he is taken to the town, passing on the way a prophet nailed to a tree, who cries:

For the freedom of the people, for the freedom of the people, for the freedom of the people—oh the starving men will live and the well-fed men will rot among the maggots of their own engendering.

And, in spite of the finery of the citizens, the "slovenly, uncared-for streets" of the town promise fulfillment of the prophecy—for when "everybody is as rich as they are, who is left to do the dirty work?" Observing the people at their state-sponsored debaucheries, Arden is himself spotted by a presently out-of-office politician, who makes him open his bag—out of which come tumbling "little men and little women, the largest of them about twelve inches long, made out of wood and carefully jointed and carved." Though he does not recognize them as his own creations, and their antics are beyond his control, they perform only at the prompting of his prologue:

> My little people in a row
> Sit on the stage and watch the show.
> The show they watch is rows and rows
> Of people watching them. Who knows
> Which is more alive than which?

Filled with frenzied rhetoric which he scarcely recognizes as his own, the Narrator thus introduces his charges: but no sooner has he finished than

without a moment's pause or hesitation they had formed themselves into two opponent groups. There was a small group of those in rich costumes, and a large group made up of the ragged and ill-favoured. Straightway the larger party flung themselves with rage upon the smaller: but were beaten back time and again by the valour of the Soldier and the duplicity of the Constable. . . . In the end the larger party were compelled to fall to their knees, abase themselves and sue for mercy.

The rest of the play reenacts just such a struggle between the fat townsfolk and the thin outsiders, on whose stolen treasures the hedonists turn out to be living: but the Narrator himself is regarded puzzledly by both parties, uncertain whether to treat his bag of theatrical tricks as an educational device or a dangerous opiate.

The mood shifts from Carroll and Swift to Kafka and back again as Arden meets a succession of dignitaries of uncertain rank, is tempted by a voluptuous concubine who turns out to be an agent for the rebellious thin men, and is finally caught up in an attack to which, the outsiders claim, the distracting displays of Arden's little men have laid them open.

I fell down upon my sack and upon the squirming heap of my terrified little men—a huge foot, shod with steel, stamped hard upon my temple. And that was the end of my dream.

The "underground cavern" that is the outsiders' retreat is transformed into a subway platform, and Arden stumbles up the escalator—to find the fat men and the thin men still all around him in the streets. He concludes:

> It would have been easy it would have been good
> To have carried a bag full of solid food
> And fed the thin men till they were
> As fat as the men who held them in fear
> But such is not in the nature of these bags
> That are given away by old women in rags.
> Such is not my nature, nor will be.
> All I can do is to look at what I see.

And it is presumably this—the artist's duty to observe and record—that just a few years later Arden was describing as "reprehensible, cowardly, and not to be imitated."

Thus, while the so-called angry young men of his generation have gradually succumbed to political disillusion, to affluent middle age, or to a conviction of the artist's impotence, Arden—who once seemed the least openly committed of them all—has arrived by his own tortuous route at an opposite conclusion. Since he has declared even his most recently performed play to be unrepresentative of his present, more militant thinking, it is, however, difficult to predict whether the balanced dialectician can transform himself into an active propagandist and still retain not his integrity—which has never been in doubt—but the qualities which have made his work to date both worthwhile and distinctive.

Arden has been an inveterate writer of prefaces: and if these have not been as long as Bernard Shaw's, it is because the plays themselves make their own substantive points. Such further gloss as Arden provides is by way of background—and also reflects his concern to offer helpful technical advice about the staging of his plays. I have myself quoted frequently from these prefaces, for in many respects Arden is his own best critic, and is certainly far more instructively aware of what his plays achieve and fail to achieve than an Osborne or a Wesker, let alone a Pinter. In part this is because he is the best craftsman of his generation—which is not necessarily to claim that he is also the best *artist,* though it argues strongly for his staying power and capacity for development. It would be as difficult to describe any one of his plays as a masterpiece as similarly to single out one of Shaw's—though there is the feeling that Arden's own *Heartbreak House* may not be all that far off. And the sheer range of his work is clearly as much more ambitious than Shaw's as it is more impressive than that of any of his contemporaries. Mannered comedy, grotesque farce, period problem play, autobiographical allegory, ballad opera, community drama, epic chronicle, mime play, melodrama—he has experimented in all these forms, and several hybrids besides, and in few has he failed outright. He has fared badly by the critics in part because of his sheer unpredictability: but he has been served well by actors and directors—surprisingly often by amateurs and student groups, as well as by professionals—because his versatility is in the best tradition of the journeyman playwright. And because he remains intensely conscious of what can and cannot be done on a stage, he has from the first been able to extend the boundaries of what is acceptable in the theatre—although, as is often the fate of pioneers, he has generally been rewarded with bafflement at the time, only to be belatedly recognized for his innovations when poetasters have made them familiar.

In attempting to sum up Arden's qualities, one still occasionally senses that a virtue may be mistaken for a vice if it goes unexplained—for each characteristic tends to throw off some unexpected and even opposite implication. It is in part because of this that one needs to have seen the more complex of the plays several times before they begin fully to reveal their riches; indeed, Arden himself once admitted, a little unhappily, that "a lot of my plays are more easily understood after a second visit." Yet it is only in an age of instant eulogy and casual condemnation that this could be regarded as a serious fault, especially since Arden's narrative skill is so sinuously strong that on a first acquaintance his plays will satisfy simply in their story-lines, a deeper understanding developing once one already *knows what happens.* Of course, a prior acquaintance with the story is implicit in the nature of chronicle plays, and Arden's acceptance and utilization of this fact may help to explain why he is the one modern playwright apart from Brecht who has been able to dramatize history into more than hopefully intellectual costume dramas. And history also lends that degree of *distance* from an action that Arden, again like Brecht, prefers to maintain—though in Arden's case this distance serves not so much Brecht's purpose of making the familiar strange as of making the strange familiar, often by suggesting a parallel that tangentially illuminates the present.

Arden is also, it follows, a civic playwright, whether his concern be with municipal housing or the politics of war and peace: but until recently his own dramatized politics, although passionate and certainly not impartial, have never been propagandist.

Now I happen to believe that art *can* make excellent propaganda, and that there is nothing intrinsically degrading in an artist choosing to enter the political arena. In ending this essay on a cautionary note, it is not, then, because I hold politics in contempt, or fail to regard the causes espoused by Arden as important. It is because, in the light of the qualities I have tried to identify, his own particular distinction as a playwright lies in a feeling for dialectics, and for the sheer complexity of the seemingly straightforward, that is usually several degrees more devastating than any direct hit aimed from one side of the polemical barricades. Arden's characters may not be as "neat and well considered" as those that tumble out of his bagman's bag — but he might do worse than bear in mind his little people's ironic warning of an attitude toward art that ultimately asserts only its impotence:

> If you bring us into battle
> You bring us only unto grief and woe
> Fracture and breakage that we cannot repair
> They will snap our wooden joints
> And pull out our cotton hair.
> Please let us please let us get back into the sack
> When the battle has been won
> We can peep out again and creep back.

The battle may not be won: but one hopes that Arden's characters — not little men, these, but ungainly, cussed, calculating, and craggy — will before very long come bursting out of his bag, their old energy reinforced by all that Arden has learnt as an artist, and experienced as a man.

SELECTED BIBLIOGRAPHY

Works of John Arden

The Waters of Babylon (1957). In Three Plays. Harmondsworth and
Baltimore, Penguin Books, 1964; New York, Grove Press, 1966.

Soldier, Soldier (1957). In Soldier, Soldier and Other Plays. London,
Methuen, 1967.

Live Like Pigs (1958). In New English Dramatists 3. Harmondsworth,
Penguin Books, 1961. Also in Three Plays. Harmondsworth and
Baltimore, Penguin Books, 1964; New York, Grove Press, 1966.

When Is a Door Not a Door? (1958). In Soldier, Soldier and Other
Plays. London, Methuen, 1967.

Serjeant Musgrave's Dance (1959). London, Methuen, 1960; New
York, Grove Press, 1962.

Wet Fish (1960). In Soldier, Soldier and Other Plays. London, Methuen,
1967.

The Happy Haven (1960). In collaboration with Margaretta D'Arcy.
In New English Dramatists 4. Harmondsworth, Penguin Books, 1962.
Also in Three Plays. Harmondsworth and Baltimore, Penguin Books,
1964; New York, Grove Press, 1966.

The Business of Good Government (1960). In collaboration with
Margaretta D'Arcy. London, Methuen, 1963; New York, Grove
Press, 1967.

Ironhand (1961). Adapted from Goethe's Goetz von Berlichingen. London, Methuen, 1965.

The Workhouse Donkey (1963). London, Methuen, 1964; New York,
Grove Press, 1967.

The True History of Squire Jonathan and His Unfortunate Treasure
(1963). In Two Autobiographical Plays. London, Methuen, 1971.

Ars Longa, Vita Brevis (1963). In collaboration with Margaretta
D'Arcy. London, Cassell, 1964.

Armstrong's Last Goodnight (1964). London, Methuen, 1965; New
York, Grove Press, 1967.

Left-Handed Liberty (1965). London, Methuen, 1965; New York,
Grove Press, 1966.

Friday's Hiding (1965). In collaboration with Margaretta D'Arcy. In
Soldier, Soldier and Other Plays. London, Methuen, 1967.

The Royal Pardon (1966). In collaboration with Margaretta D'Arcy.
London, Methuen, 1967.

The Hero Rises Up (1968). In collaboration with Margaretta D'Arcy.
London, Methuen, 1969.

The Bagman; or, The Impromptu of Muswell Hill (1969). In Two Autobiographical Plays. London, Methuen, 1971.

Critical Works and Commentary

Brandt, G. W. "Realism and Parable: From Brecht to Arden." In Contemporary Theatre, ed. John Russell Brown and Bernard Harris. Stratford-upon-Avon Studies, Vol. IV, pp. 33–55. London, Edward Arnold, 1962.

Gaskill, William. "Producing Arden: An Interview with Tom Milne," *Encore*, XII, No. 5 (September–October, 1965), 20–26.

Gilman, Richard. "Arden's Unsteady Ground," *Tulane Drama Review*, XI, No. 2 (1966), 54–62.

Hainsworth, J. D. "John Arden," *Hibbert Journal*, LXV (Autumn, 1966), 25–27.

Hoffman, Theodore. "Reconnoitering Arden's 'War,'" *Educational Theatre Journal*, XIX (1967), 509–10.

Hunt, Albert. "Arden's Stagecraft," *Encore*, XII, No. 5 (September–October, 1965), 9–12.

Hunt, Albert, and Geoffrey Reeves. "Arden: Professionals and Amateurs," *Encore*, XII, No. 5 (September–October, 1965), 27–36.

Kitchin, Laurence. Drama in the Sixties: Form and Interpretation. London, Faber, 1966. See "Epic as Drama: Arden," pp. 85–89.

Manchester, Victoria. "Let's Do Some More Undressing: The 'War Carnival' at New York University," *Educational Theatre Journal*, XIX (1967), 502–9.

Marowitz, Charles. "The Workhouse Donkey." In The Encore Reader, ed. Charles Marowitz et al., pp. 238–41. London, Methuen, 1965.

Mills, John. "Love and Anarchy in *Serjeant Musgrave's Dance*," *Drama Survey*, VII (1969), 45–51.

Milne, Tom. "The Hidden Face of Violence." In The Encore Reader, ed. Charles Marowitz et al., pp. 115–24. London, Methuen, 1965.

Page, Malcolm. "The Motives of Pacifists: Arden's *Serjeant Musgrave*," *Drama Survey*, VI (1967), 66–73.

Rush, David. "Grief, but Good Order," *Moderna Språk*, LVIII (1964), 452–58.

Shrapnel, Susan. "John Arden and the Public Stage," *Cambridge Quarterly*, IV (Summer, 1969), 225–36.

Taylor, John Russell. *Anger and After*. London, Methuen, 1969. See "Presented at Court: John Arden," pp. 83–105.

Tindale, Joan Blindheim. "John Arden's Use of the Stage," *Modern Drama*, XI (1968), 306–16.

Trussler, Simon. "Political Progress of a Paralyzed Liberal: The Community Dramas of John Arden," *Tulane Drama Review*, XIII, No. 4 (1969), 181–91.

Watson, Ian. "Kirbymoorside '63, with a Footnote by John Arden," *Encore*, X, No. 6 (November–December, 1963), 17–21.